GRIMOIRE GALAXY

Liza Jill Meyers

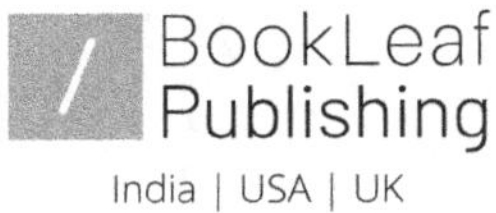

BookLeaf Publishing

India | USA | UK

Presentation by *BookLeaf Publishing*

Web: www.bookleafpub.com

E-mail: info@bookleafpub.com

ISBN: 9789363319936

First edition 2021

Sending love from afar, today, tomorrow, and always, to all those watching over me; over the rainbow and beyond the milky way.

"The windows are illuminated by the evening/ Sunshine through them, fiery gems/ for you, only for you."

— Crosby, Stills, Nash & Young

"Picture the fire still burning, except now it's beyond the horizon. A sunset."

— Chuck Palahniuk

My Roots Bloom to Bouquets

My Mom gives me the words and passion
Teaching me through craft and creativity

My Dad gives me the music and rhythm
Passing his talent for melody and lyricism

My Sister gives me the stars and freedom
Instilling the independence to be myself

My Cousins give me make believe and imagination
Sandbox pretending, spontaneous silliness, and dress up

My Boyfriend gives me realism and grounds me back to Earth
When I am spiraling away and need a bungee cord

My Nona gives me strength and courage
To face hard obstacles in life with grace

MYSTICISMS

PREFACE

My boyfriend in high school casually remarked, "Don't you write any happy poems?" which has subconsciously sat with me for decades. Poems of levity and light always seemed too cliché and trite. (I was also a teenager fulfilling my "woe is me" role.) But he was right! My poems were littered with somber sorrow and hyperbolic dramatic darkness. (As an aside, however, I would just like to say that the idea of more morose poems being alarming or depressed, is a stigma that we should do our best to rid; after all, Emily Dickinson made a whole career out of the macabre.) So, with that said, I have been pleasantly surprised with the sheer joy that this collection oozes. Even when commenting on grief, trauma, or the loss of a loved one, I strived for the tug on the heartstrings. And even in my more descriptive pieces, I sought out meaning with positive perceptions.

Crunching out 20 poems in 20 days, after a three-year (plus) drought, felt like too steep a challenge (like the stairs in my Aunt and Uncle's old abode). And even though the flow started out as a trickle, I'd say it ended in a waterfall surge. And still, I pushed myself in other ways: selecting two-word titles for each piece (save for one special one), interspersing form poetry throughout (such as a haiku, a pantoum, and a play on a sonnet), as well as assigning brackets of my lineup to the four seasons (1/2/19/20: spring; 3-8: summer; 9- 14: autumn; 15-18: winter). But the greatest, and most unexpected challenge was losing my grandfather in the midst of this feat. In fact, the majority of this book was written in the aftermath of his passing. But through these poems, it has been such a benefit to have a daily outlet where I can suss through mourning and memories.

While not every poem displays these motifs (as several are based on my relationship with my current boyfriend of over three years, my rotten scoundrel), I have memorialized members of my family, as well as a dear friend, who are no longer with me. That same dear friend, Ray (and he was one hell of a ray of sunshine), once shared, "Life begins at the end of your comfort zone," which fits me perfectly; as the horizon has always been an endless infinity to me, where anything is possible. I have always been keen on the idea of the horizon line being a curtain I can peer behind. And behind this curtain is a world of vibrantly rich colors, cool pools, lush fields, and a purple, pink, orange, yellow sunset.

And I did just that; that is, exploring the limits of my comfort zone. Through this writing, I am now on the other side of the horizon's stage, skipping in a field, because I managed to achieve happiness in all this poetry you will now read. The irony is, I was born with a smile on my face, which dubbed me "Happy Head" to my parents, and am very much an optimistic person.

So my ex-boyfriend was really wrong about me. Cause Happy Head is free and she is wandering without misery.

So now, I leave you with this tidbit: the
best advice I ever received was to simply
"SMILE"; if you cast this one spell daily, I
assure you that you will float gravityless
in your own galaxy.

Spring

1.

Cosmic Waltz

Once upon a time
I'd be a princess
Spinning in a yellow dress
With polka dots and orange accents
I'd be the sun
And his face in the sun
Blonde strands glinting to gold
Blue eyes squinting
Him leaning close
Him lean and tall
With a Star Wars smile
I'd sigh with desire
To tiptoe up
And kiss him
And I'll kiss him
Overlooking a castle
Spinning in a purple dress
With black straps and gold sequin
And he'll kiss me as we dance
Like we are flying
Past all constellations
And I'll make a crown out of stars

2.

SPIRAL FLOWERS

curve into a bloom
pushing petals off like jewels
we used to sing, "he loves me"
with forget-me-nots
like dandelion fuzz
blown in summer
pollen sprinkling the wind
springing baby's breath
in a spittle plume

Summer

3.

Nebular Daydream

Swimming with the clouds
Diving through their mist
Like dolphins leaping
Above crystallized oceans
In the brushes of boat bubbles
And splashes of seafoam

4.

Lady Lillian

She sits in her lawn chair
At the foot of the grass
Our tree with the turned trunk
Beside her waving hand

She shimmers in a stream
Beaming a sheer glow gleam
A square smile spread
To the dimples of her cheeks
Pursed mouth and cupid-bow lips

Her hair is a soft cotton bed of curls
Tufts tucked like a pearl tiara
My hair layers the same fabric
My smile cut in the same shape

I see her as she dreams of elephants
With sprouting noses like a sprinkler
Us running through the fountain water
As we circle around her winding time
Conjuring her laughter in strokes of summer

5.

Midnight Storm

Lightening branches
Caught in flashes
Electric energy
Purple jolts igniting
A blaze of bang-snap bursts
In a ring around
The cul-de-sac

Along the lane in neon freckles
Bulbs of fire flare
Twinkle-bites in twilight
Snatching night bugs
To illuminate lanterns
Shedding shade from shadows
With puddles of prism light

6.

Grandpa Vegas

All that's left is a band of gold

He paces in white socks
On linoleum floors
That slip and slide from ammonia
Which can give you a pneumonia
If you breathe it in day and night
And at night he paces
Fraught dreams of snapshots
That look like Polaroids
Exposing excerpts from his life
Colors fading to black and white
A Korean War fight or a gaslight
And in the night he takes delight
In his beloved redhead with painted nails
In a tennis court or a golf cart
In the multicolor glass flowers like a mosaic
And the fountain cascading waves
In their hands firmly clasped
Fingers intertwining
And their gold bands
Tinkling together his broken heart

7.

Enchantment Grove

I scatter my memories on a cookie sheet
and bake them in the oven till they shrink.
And when they chill, I collect them in a picnic basket —
small red berries, or mini pin cherries,
the ones I associated with rabies as a kid —
to enter the forest of wild things.

Along the path, I toss handfuls of dewberries
throughout the meadow. I see them sink
and each root sprouts instantly, a stalk;
but I skip along further into the woods,
dropping more berries like a flower girl down the aisle.

At a verge of the course, cozy in its weeds,
a cottage of cobblestone with a cauldron alight.
A witchy lady, with slender hands and skinny fingers,
reaches out to me in a crawl and shrieks,

"Why do you destroy your fruit in this manner?
Throwing to the foot of the forest, littering like garbage?"

I clutch my basket tighter and watch her stir.
Behind me, the forest is a lush and vibrant woodland;
velvet fronds in a shimmering pine cast an orb
above me. Whirring, whipping, whizzing —
I faint blinking, behold a lattice of ruffles,
like puzzle pieces that nearly fit to each.

Each hole, here in this pattern, though, a dewdrop,

which sprinkle upon my cheeks and soak

my eyelashes. Which sneak into my pores

like glitter fragments from a firework,

dusting the air, drifting, descending

in a sugar spill upon my head.

Spreading saccharine sap to soil the ground again.

8.

Stellar Sunset

I saw the precipice as swirls
With bright starry eyes
Brilliant blue hues of hidden scars
Striped swipes and paisley spirals
Curls that drip in spills of yellow
Orange frills of radiance
Periwinkle wind swishing
Billowing bright bulbs
Pulsing like flickering fireflies
And bouncing in the gloam
A cluster of celestial crystals
Resiliently burning and sparking

I peel back the curtain of the horizon
to see ombre blending in bolting rays

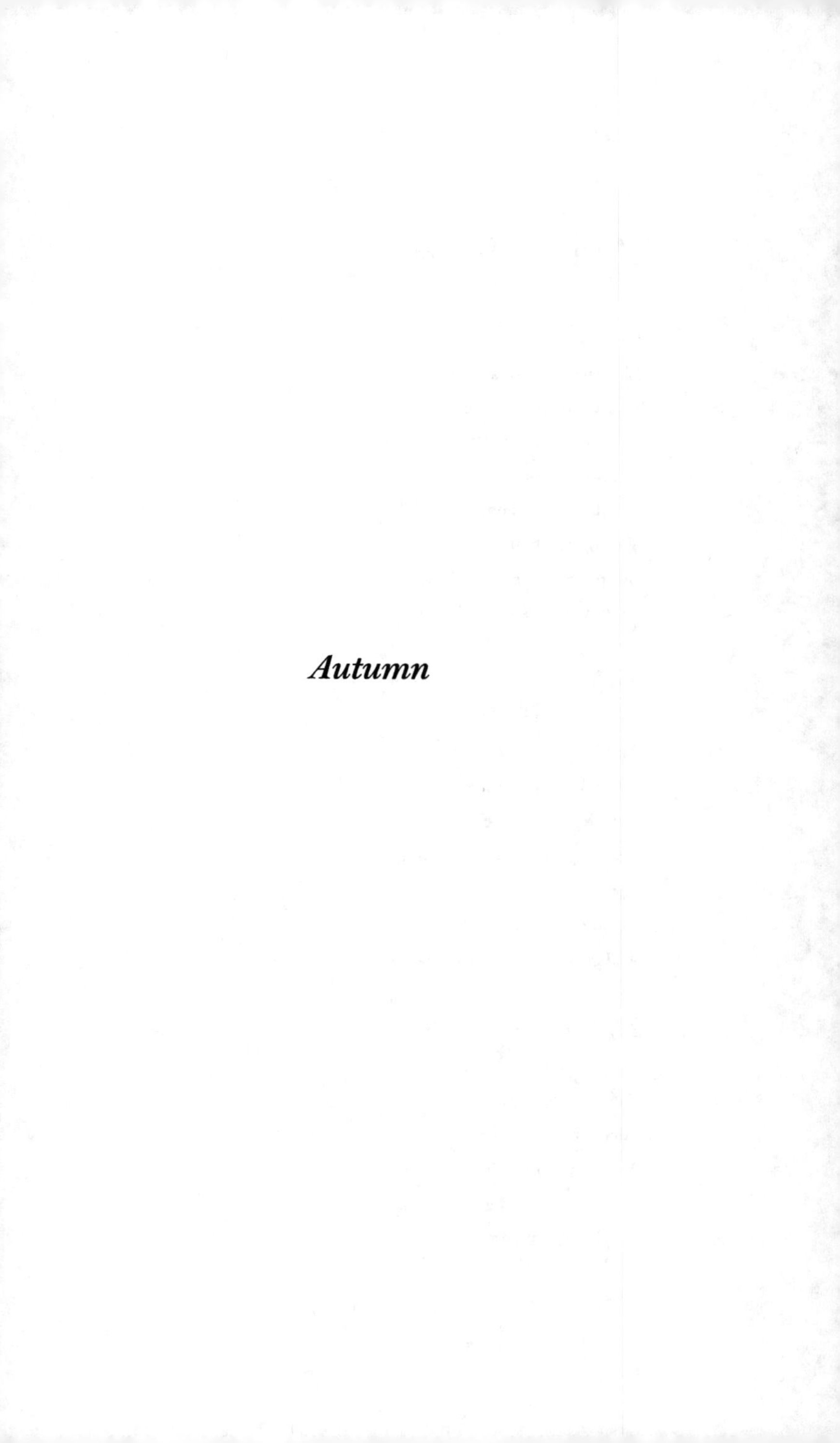

Autumn

9.

Mourning Evergreen

Grief layers
Like the rings of a tree
Scar tissue hardening
Rough tree-trunk bark
In knotted rope
Climbing each rung
To ring the bell at the spire
But my hands are slipping
And my hands burn through

Again I ascend
With flatfooted converses
And I reach out to you
Cause I feel like I might detach
If we let go and I go freefalling
Crashing down to Earth and sprawling
Appendages in the grass
My parachute exploding
And chords snapping in half

So grab my hand and hoist
Me back up to your branch
Where we can share
Sticky sandwiches
And stare through binoculars
At leaves shedding
Stirring chromatically

Cocooning colors

And soaring into butterflies

10.

Synchronous heartbeat

Satin pillow chats

Cuddles pressed into your chest

Remnants of your scent

11.

The Library

Books waft in mahogany
A musk of stacked pages
Birchwood breeze sauntering in the air
Through two doors as bookends
Upon a haunting silence of fluorescents

Across from me sits my redheaded friend
She prattles faraway
Muffled whispers in a tunnel
And in this echo-chamber cave
Clocks do not possess their hands
Hearing distorts to warped deafness

I see an old man in plaid
Floating across the threshold
Resembling a past professor
He shuffles along shelves and rows
Blurring by spines and spindles
Slipping behind a green chalkboard
Erasing through its backside
Fading beyond the corner of time
And leaving rustling leaves burning
Cedar incense in the wake of his aroma

12.

Love Link

One hand curves
as half a heart
another mirroring
like a friendship
necklace clicking
grooves and ridges
fragments merging
mending and forging
scoops of scallops
like a lover's caress
arms clasped
in winking couplets

13.

Shriveled Bouquets

Dead flowers crinkle
Hanging upside down —
Bats sleeping in a cave
Or inverted crosses
Twisted in their faith —
Blooming nightshade
In a dusty perfume
Mummified in cobwebs
For eternal decay

14.

Lighthouse Lullaby

Waves whisper languidly
Lightly licking the shore
The tide a sweet swish
Sparkling saltwater
Where the lighthouse stands
A beacon
A bulb
An orb
its spotlight sways
Beams along the sand

The water shuffles
Seafoam brushes
Curling surf surging
A swelling deluge
Raging in a roar
Crashing combers
Against the watchtower

Imprinting the seaboard
Sunken footprints
Sailors rush
From crushed ships
A stampede twirling
Round spiral stairs
Winding squalling wind
A siren's wail

Sprouting deep within
The whorling whirlpool
Erupting through the storm

An eye roaming
The lighthouse socket spins
its globe
A bulb
An orb
Harboring the mourning
Sun rising from the shining
Surface of glistening sea
Lapping the sands gently
With salty ripples
Kissing tickles

Winter

15.

So long, Adam

Nona's kitchen feels like a fireplace
Where my Uncle bent a spoon to prove he could
And made me belt, "Beautiful" in the living room
But the last time I saw him was his birthday

I still have the spoon you squeezed together
Bending it with your bare hands, inward, on its head
The last time I saw you was your birthday
Somehow you didn't seem happy then

I had a dream of your hand reaching outward from the ground
Like a flower rooted in cement, sprouting upward
Forebodingly telling me something was unsaid
But you told me to always keep ahead, looking forward

You are now a breeze drifting through the world
So I sang, "Wind Beneath My Wings" at your wake
Surging upward, linking arms, always moving forward
Nona's home is the hearthstone where we heal your name

16.

Sapphire Archer

Oh celestial centaur
With the alluring albedo —

Rising with the day
Elliptic blue eyes
Reflect and refract rays —
Frozen snowflakes
Galaxies of glass —
Violet flames of ice
Shot by the bow of Sagittarius

Waning with the moon
Midnight blue masks the stars
As clouds blur in a fog —
Shuffling solstice refrains
Of "Blue on Blue"
As navy zebras gallop
Frost through snowy terrain

17.

Yuletide Tinge

What does Merry Christmas mean
When you can't see red and green?

A Film Noir Festivity —
Multicolored lights blinking
In splotches of gray
Like slushy sleet
Sloshing in city streets —

Sepia poinsettias
In decorated vases
Frame a bleached display —
Stocking stuffers turn to beige
As tinsel loses tincture —
This dazzling spectacular
A palette of charcoal haze
So why not sleigh into a snowflake
Iridescent icicles will hail your faith!

18.

Supernova Shuttle

The crowd gathered at 9am
Huddled close for heat
The chill had been evaporating
But lingered in visible breath
Eager children with clasped hands
Rosy cheeked with anxiety
2 hours till the launchpad

6 astronauts and a teacher
Prepare for their postponed
Mission in a cluster prayer
"Ride, Sally, Ride"
Echoing in their mind
The ignition whirring
A frostbitten crack
Coated in dry ice
No one hears on the tarmac

Countdown Commence
T-minus
10
9
8
7
6
5
4

3

2

1

Blast off!

The rocket blazes like a bullet

A frostquake rupturing

Flourishing a fountain firework

A cozy comet explosion

Of snowflake freckles

Scattering on upward

Faces of children

Tongues out

Glee fleeting

"I stand outside

with my mouth open wide"

The crowd hushed at 11:45

Mouths agape in downturned frowns

A flurry of debris

Drifting into their eyelashes

Blinding the flight

Plummeting to the ground

Spring

19.

Farewell, Wanderer

She spies clouds shifting
In their stratus mist
A lethargic cumulus
Titans striking fists
Slow-motion rumbles
Bolting thunder on Mount Olympus

She cartwheels windmills
Twirling a tap dance on train tracks
Undergrowth spoking between each plank
Unfurling jewelweed maple seed
Sap sticking like scotch tape
Bejeweling her snout like de Bergerac

She leaps onto a rolling freight
Stargazes through carriage doors
As constellations wane
Orion chasing seven sisters
Their orbit fading
Waterfalling into ombre

She dips her toe in the pupil of the sky
And swims upstream
In the pool of its iris
And hops along hills of jade
Ripping apart four-leaf clovers
As she dreams in the sunset glaze

20.

Fairytale Whirlwind

Rapunzel
Unpins her locks
And tumbles down her tower
Splayed in a hammock
Of her braided hair
Cords of rope dangling
Where princes
Once stumbled up rungs
Reaching the climb
Ringing chimes
With a princess kiss
Like an acrobat
She twirls her silk
Unfurling satin strands
Spilling at her ankles
Once she stands
Wobbling in a waddle
Her sea legs flail
Somersaults in the grass
She collapses
Scraping nails
In crescents of dirt
Hurling her body
In butterfly strokes
Until she reaches a bank
Of sandcastles
Smashing moats

As she dives

Splashing in a tie-dye tide

Shimmer of the eye

Sinking in seaweed

A quicksand suction

Drowning in the whirlpool

Floundering in the ocean

Until she flourishes

Like a spraying fountain

An emerald siren

Singing her mermaid melody

She rises in a surge

Crashing the surface

Dipping into the face of the sea

As the sun melts the horizon

And she ebbs into the abyss

Submerging one flipper

Scales of sequins

In the distance

Like a dolphin flapping

Wings waving farewell

With her tale

Fin